Stage 2

On the Road

Donn Byrne
Illustrated by
Mervyn Suart

revised impression

Longman
Structural
Readers

Part One

This is the road to the city. It is a big road and there are cars and trucks on it. The cars and trucks are going to the city. The city is six hundred kilometres from here.

This is a small village in the mountains. It is nearly twenty kilometres from the road. The people in this village are poor and their houses are small.

This house is in the village. It is small but there is a large family in it. There are eight people in the family.

The woman is crying. She says to the man: "We don't have any money. Our children are hungry and I don't have any food for them."

The man is looking at his family. He is sad. His children are hungry. What can he do for them? There isn't any work for him in the village and he can't get money there.

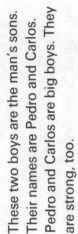

The man says to the woman: "I can go to the big city and I can find work there. There's work in the city. I can't stay here. What can I do in the village?"

These two boys are the man's sons. Their names are Pedro and Carlos. Pedro and Carlos are big boys. They are strong, too.

The two boys say to their father: "Can you take us with you? We're big and strong, and we can work in the city, too."

Their father answers them: "I can take one son with me. I can't take two. Which one of you will come?"

Pedro takes his father's hand and says: "Take me, Father. Carlos can look after the family." Carlos says: "No, father. Leave Pedro here. He can look after the family."

The man has two pieces of paper and he has written the word YES on the first piece. Now he is writing NO on the second piece.

Now the two pieces are in his hat. The man says to his sons: "Shut your eyes. Put your hand into my hat and take out one piece of paper."

Carlos takes a piece of paper out of the hat and looks at it. He says: "The word NO is on my piece." Carlos is very sad because he cannot go with his father.

Pedro looks at his piece of paper. He says: "The word YES is on my piece. I can come with you, Father." Pedro is very happy.

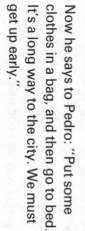

The man says to Carlos: "Be a good son, Carlos. Stay here and look after your mother. Look after your sisters, too. Pedro and I must go to the city."

Now he says to Pedro: "Put some clothes in a bag, and then go to bed. It's a long way to the city. We must get up early."

Part Two

Now it is morning. The sun is coming up behind the mountains. Pedro and his father are leaving their home. Carlos is standing near his mother. She is crying.

Pedro and his father are walking to the big road. Pedro's father has a bag on his back. There are some clothes and a little food in it. Pedro is carrying a small bag.

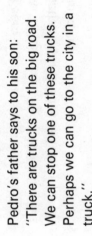

Pedro's father says to his son: "There are trucks on the big road. We can stop one of these trucks. Perhaps we can go to the city in a truck."

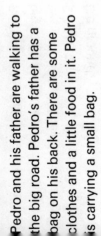

Pedro's father can see the big road. He points at it and says: "Look, Pedro. Look down there. What can you see?"

Pedro answers: "I can see the big road. It's the road to the city. Look at the trucks on it." Pedro is pointing at the trucks.

Pedro and his father are running. to the big road. Pedro is holding his father's hand. They are very near the road now.

Pedro and his father have run to the big road. Now they are standing beside the road. They are waiting for a truck. They have put their bags on the ground.

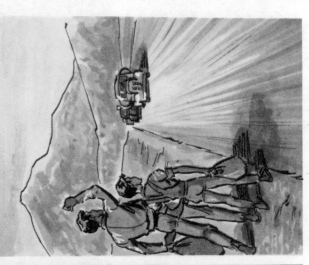

Pedro and his father are waiting for a truck. Pedro points and says: "Look, Father. A big truck is coming now. Can you stop it?" Pedro's father raises his hand.

The truck is near Pedro and his father. The driver can see them but he is not going to stop. He is going along the road very quickly.

Two trucks are coming down the road. Pedro's father has raised his hand again. He says: "Stop! Stop! Take us to the city."

The first truck does not stop. But the second truck is stopping in front of Pedro and his father. They take their bags and run to the truck.

The driver puts his head out of the window. He says to Pedro's father: "Do you have any money? It's a long way to the city. I want some money from you."

Pedro's father says: "I'm a poor man. I don't have any money. You have a truck and you are going to the city. Be kind and take us with you."

There are cars and trucks on the road, but they do not stop. Pedro's father does not raise his hand again. He has taken his bag and he is putting it on his back.

The truck is moving again but Pedro and his father are not in it. The driver is not going to take them to the city. They are very sad.

Part Three

Pedro and his father are walking down the road. It is afternoon. The sun is over their heads, so they are hot and tired. They are hungry, too.

A big truck is coming down the road, Pedro can see it. He is thinking: "I can't walk to the city. I must stop this truck. I will run in front of it. It's not going very quickly."

Pedro is standing in the middle of the road. He has raised his hands. He says: "Stop! Stop! Take us to the city."

The driver of the truck thinks: "This man and his son are tired. I have a big truck, so I can take them to the city."

Pedro and his father are standing beside the truck. Pedro's father is talking to the driver. "Can you take us to the city? We don't have any money."

The driver says: "Yes, I can take you. You can't walk to the city. It's a long way. Get into the truck and sit beside me. Your son can sit in the back. He can sit on the boxes."

Pedro is getting into the truck. His father is helping him. There is a place for Pedro between the boxes.

The truck is moving again. Pedro's father is sitting beside the driver and he is talking to him: "What are you carrying on your truck? What's in those boxes?" he asks.

"There's fruit in the boxes," the driver says. "It's from my farm. I'm taking it to the city. There isn't any fruit there. I can sell my fruit in the city."

Pedro's father watches the driver of the truck. He watches the driver's hands and feet. Pedro's father cannot drive, but he is learning.

The driver answers: "Yes, you can get work there. Can you drive a truck? It isn't hard. Watch me and you can learn."

"That's good," Pedro's father says. "You can sell your fruit in the city and you can get money for it. Is there work in the city? Can I find work for my son and me?"

Pedro is very happy. He is sitting on the boxes and he is looking at the land. He thinks: "We're going to the city. We're going in a truck!"

The sun is going down. Night is coming. The driver says: "Night is coming, and I'm tired. We have come a long way. There's a nice place near here and we can stop there."

The truck is not on the road now. It is beside the road between two trees. The driver is lighting a fire and Pedro's father is helping him. Pedro has got some wood for the fire.

They have a big fire and there is a pot on it. The driver has put some food in the pot and is cooking it. Pedro's father is looking in his bag.

Pedro's father has a little food in his hand. It is from his bag. "I have some food, too," he says to the driver. "Take it." But the driver does not take the food.

The driver is sleeping, but Pedro's father is looking at the driver. He is not tired. He can watch and the driver can sleep. Pedro is sleeping under the truck.

Part Four

Pedro's father is sitting beside the fire. He is watching. He can hear the noise of animals. They are in the trees but they do not come near the fire.

It is morning. The driver and Pedro's father have cups in their hands and they are drinking. Pedro asks his father: "Can I sit beside the driver?"

Pedro's father says: "Yes, Pedro. You can sit beside the driver. I'm tired now. I can go in the back and I can sleep there."

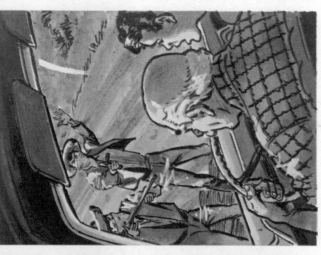

Pedro is sitting beside the driver. The driver is talking to him. The truck is moving quickly. There aren't any cars or trucks on the road.

There are two men on the road. They have guns in their hands. They are robbers.

The tall robber is standing in the middle of the road. He has raised his hand. The short robber points his gun at the truck. "Stop!" they say. "Stop your truck!"

The truck has stopped. The driver puts his head out of the window. He speaks to the robbers. "What do you want?" he says. "You can't stop my truck."

The tall robber says: "We can stop your truck because we have guns. Now get out of the truck and go to those trees. Be quick!" He is pointing his gun at the driver.

Pedro and the driver are walking to the trees. The trees are near the road. The driver has put his hands up. The two robbers are following them.

Pedro's father is not sleeping now. He is watching the robbers. He can't help the driver and his son because the robbers have guns. He doesn't have a gun.

The short robber takes a piece of rope and he ties the driver to a tree. The rope is very strong. The tall robber is holding Pedro's arm. He has his gun in his hand and he is pointing it at the driver.

Now the short robber is tying Pedro to a tree. There is a cloth in Pedro's mouth and he cannot speak. He cannot move and he cannot make any noise. There is a cloth in the driver's mouth, too.

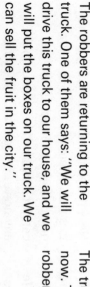

The robbers are returning to the truck. One of them says: "We will drive this truck to our house, and we will put the boxes on our truck. We can sell the fruit in the city."

The truck is at the robbers' house now. Their truck is there, too. The robbers are going into their house.

This room is in the robbers' house. There are some bottles on the table. The robbers have glasses in their hands and they are drinking.

Pedro's father is getting off the truck. He thinks: "Where are the robbers now? What are they doing? Are their guns in their hands?"

Pedro's father is standing at the window and he is looking into the room. He can see the robbers but they cannot see him. They are drinking. Their guns are not in their hands.

Pedro's father is thinking: "There are men in the village near here. They can help me. I can drive the truck to the village."

26

Pedro's father is looking at the robbers' truck. He thinks: "The robbers will follow me in their truck, but I can stop them. I can cut a hole in the tire."

Pedro's father is beside the wheel. He has cut the tire with his knife. He is making a big hole in it. The robbers cannot follow him now.

Pedro's father has got into the truck and he is driving it from the house. "I watched the driver and now I can drive," he thinks. "I am going to drive the truck to the village."

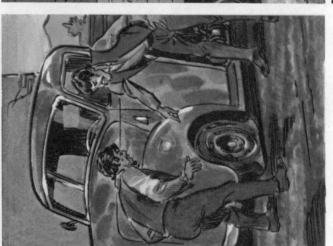

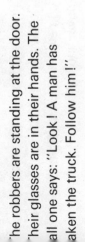

The robbers are standing at the door. Their glasses are in their hands. The tall one says: "Look! A man has taken the truck. Follow him!"

The robbers are near their truck. One of them is pointing at the wheel. "Look!" he says. "There's a hole in the tire. We can't follow him now."

Part Five

Pedro's father has arrived at the village. He is telling his story to a policeman. "You must go quickly and arrest the robbers. They can't drive their truck. There's a hole in the tire."

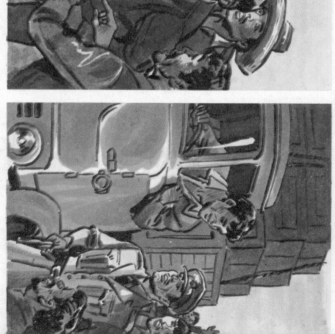

The men are saying to the policeman: "Yes, go and arrest the robbers. They are bad men. They have guns but we have guns, too. We will help you."

Pedro's father is in the truck again. He says to the policeman: "I can't come with you. I must find the driver and my son."

Pedro's father has arrived at the trees near the road. He is running to the driver and his son. He is calling to them. They can see him but they cannot answer. There are cloths in their mouths.

Pedro's father has taken his knife and he has cut the rope round Pedro's hands and feet. Pedro can move now. Then his father goes to the driver and cuts the rope round him, too.

Pedro's father and the driver walk to the truck. Pedro's father is telling his story. "The policeman and his men are at the house now. They will arrest the robbers."

Pedro's father and the driver are in the village again. The policeman and his men are there, too. The robbers are standing beside the policeman's car. The policeman is tying the tall robber to the short robber.

Now they have left the village and are going to the city. "You're a good man," the driver says to Pedro's father. "You can work for me. You can work on my farm and you can drive my truck. You must write to your wife and tell her."

Pedro and his father have arrived in the city. They are in a room there. Pedro is sleeping. His father is writing a letter. He is writing to his wife.

This is the letter: "I have a good friend now. He has a farm and a truck. We can live on the farm and I can work there. Leave the village. Come quickly and bring the children."

The man's wife is reading the letter to her children. "Your father has work. He has work on a farm. We can go to the farm and we can live there, too." She and the children are very happy.

THE END

Exercises

A. Look at these sentences:

The man **is writing** NO on this piece of paper.
The man **has written** YES on this piece of paper.

Now finish the second sentence in the same way:

1. Carlos is taking a piece of paper out of the hat.
   Pedro _____ a piece of paper out of the hat.
2. Pedro is putting his bag on the ground.
   His father _____ his bag by a stone.
3. Pedro is picking up his bag.
   His father _____ his bag.
4. The driver is getting on the truck.
   Pedro and his father _____ the truck.
5. The sun is going down.
   The sun _____ down.

B. Look at these sentences:

I don't have _____ clothes. I don't have **any** clothes.
I have _____ clothes. I have **some** clothes.

Now finish these sentences. Put **some** or **any**.

1. He doesn't have _____ money.
2. There are _____ clothes in the bag.
3. I have _____ food.
4. There aren't _____ cars on the road.
5. They have _____ wood for the fire.
6. There isn't _____ work for him.

C. Look at these sentences:

A house is in the village.
There is a house in the village.

Now finish the second sentence:

1. Some clothes are in the bag.
   _____ some clothes in the bag.
2. A big truck is coming.
   _____ a big truck coming.
3. Two trees are beside the road.
   _____ two trees beside the road.

D. This is a question: **Can he drive a truck?**

This is the answer (YES): **Yes, he can** drive a truck.
This is the answer (NO): **No, he can't** drive a truck.

Now finish the answers to the questions.

1. Question: Can he get work in the city?
   Answer (YES): _____ get work in the city.
2. Question: Can Carlos go with his father?
   Answer (NO): _____ go with his father.
3. Question: Can they go to the city in a truck?
   Answer (YES): _____ go to the city in a truck.
4. Question: Can Pedro sit beside the driver?
   Answer (YES): _____ can sit beside the driver.
5. Question: Can they walk to the city?
   Answer (NO): _____ walk to the city.

E. Look at these sentences:

They have put **their bags** on the ground.
They have put **them** on the ground.

Now change these sentences in the same way. Put **him, her, it** or **them**.

1. The driver is not going to take **Pedro and his father** to the city.
2. He is pointing **his gun** at the driver.
3. I can take **this man and his son** to the city.
4. You must write to **your wife**.
5. Pedro's father is looking at **the robbers' truck**.
6. Stay here and look after **your mother**.
7. The driver is talking to **Pedro**.
8. I don't have any food for **the children**.

4. A truck is near Pedro and his father.
   _____ a truck near Pedro and his father.
5. Two men are on the road.
   _____ two men on the road.
6. Animals are in the trees.
   _____ animals in the trees.